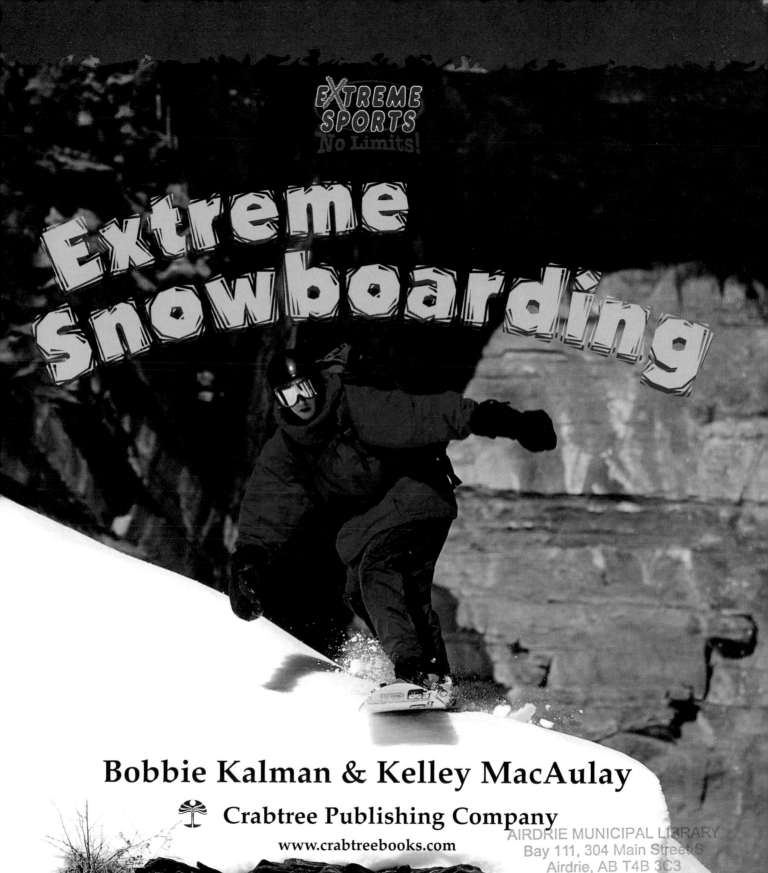

EXTREME
SPORTS
No Limits!

Extreme Snowboarding

Bobbie Kalman & Kelley MacAulay

Crabtree Publishing Company

www.crabtreebooks.com

Created by Bobbie Kalman

Dedicated by Kelley MacAulay
For Kyle Bellamy, the coolest boy I know

Editor-in-Chief
Bobbie Kalman

Writing team
Bobbie Kalman
Kelley MacAulay

Substantive editor
Amanda Bishop

Project editor
Kelley MacAulay

Editors
Molly Aloian
Rebecca Sjonger
Kathryn Smithyman

Art director
Robert MacGregor

Design
Katherine Kantor

Production coordinator
Heather Fitzpatrick

Photo research
Crystal Foxton

Consultant
Tom Collins, Executive Director,
United States of America Snowboarding Association (USASA)

Special thanks to
Burton Snowboards, Sherman Poppen

Photographs
Burton Snowboards: pages 5, 19, 20, 22, 24, 25, 28, 29, 30
© Sherman Poppen: pages 6, 7
AP/Wide World Photos: pages 14, 15
Philippe Millereau.DPPI/Icon SMI: page 13
Manna Photography: © Judy Manna: pages 17, 26, 31
Chris Kelly/Photosport.com: page 18
Shazamm: page 27
Other images by Adobe Image Library, Corbis Images, and PhotoDisc

Illustrations
Katherine Kantor: pages 10, 21
Rob MacGregor: pages 8-9
Bonna Rouse: page 11

Digital prepress
Embassy Graphics

Printer
Worzalla Publishing Company

Crabtree Publishing Company

www.crabtreebooks.com   1-800-387-7650

PMB 16A	612 Welland Avenue	73 Lime Walk
350 Fifth Avenue	St. Catharines	Headington
Suite 3308	Ontario	Oxford
New York, NY	Canada	OX3 7AD
10118	L2M 5V6	United Kingdom

Cataloging-in-Publication Data
Kalman, Bobbie.
  Extreme snowboarding / Bobbie Kalman & Kelley MacAulay.
    p. cm. -- (Extreme sports no limits series)
  Includes index.
  ISBN 0-7787-1672-4 (RLB) -- ISBN 0-7787-1718-6 (pbk.)
  1. Snowboarding--Juvenile literature. 2. Extreme sports. [1. Snowboarding. 2. Extreme sports.] I. MacAulay, Kelley. II. Title. III. Extreme sports no limits!
  GV857.S57K35 2003
  796.93--dc22
                                                              2003025587
                                                              LC

CONTENTS

EXTREME SNOWBOARDING

Snowboarding is a combination of surfing and skiing. It is one of the world's fastest growing **extreme sports**. In extreme sports, athletes defy expectations and push their sports to the very limit. **Professional** or "pro" snowboarders make a living from snowboarding. They train for years to become the best **riders**, or snowboarders, they can be. Snowboarding is also an **individual sport**, which means that athletes perform alone. Although pro riders compete individually, many belong to teams, which are **sponsored** by companies that design and make snowboards and gear.

SO MANY STYLES

There are three main styles of extreme snowboarding: **alpine**, **freestyle**, and **freeride**. Alpine snowboarding is all about racing—riders attempt to cross a finish line with the best time. Freestyle riders perform thrilling **tricks**, or moves, on their boards. Freeride is not about competing at all. Instead, snowboarders hike up **backcountry** mountains so they can ride on untouched slopes.

BOARDER CULTURE

Snowboarding has its own **culture**. A culture is a set of values that a group of people share. Snowboarding culture is similar to that of other extreme sports such as BMX biking, skateboarding, and in-line skating. It includes its own **lingo**, or language, and clothing styles. Many extreme riders enjoy hip-hop and alternative music—in fact, it is often played very loudly during competitions! Some riders also own companies that make boards, gear, and baggy clothing that appeal to a snowboarder's relaxed sense of style.

EXTREME DANGER

The pictures in this book show pros pulling off exciting stunts that may be tempting to try. Remember that these tricks take years to master. Only professionals should attempt extreme snowboarding.

SNURFING U.S.A.

The very first snowboard wasn't a snowboard—it was a **Snurfer**! In 1965, an American named Sherman Poppen invented the Snurfer when he bolted together two skis and later attached a rope to the front end. The toy's name combined the words "snow" and "surfer." Surfing was a popular sport in America in the 1960s, but not all kids lived near an ocean. Snurfing became a way for kids to try surfing on snow instead of on water.

GAINING CONTROL

In 1977, Jake Burton designed a board that had foot **bindings**. Bindings allowed riders to **maneuver**, or control, the board easily. Burton called his new invention a snowboard. The snowboard soon replaced the Snurfer in America. Before long, companies started using **ski technology** to make snowboards lighter, faster, and more flexible.

Poppen made the first Snurfer (shown above) for his daughter. It was a huge hit with the neighborhood kids!

NEW OPPORTUNITIES

Terry Kidwell, the "father of freestyle," was among a group of teenagers in Lake Tahoe, California who put the new boards to the test. He and his friends carved a **halfpipe**, or U-shaped ditch, out of the snow behind the city dump and began trying skateboarding tricks on it with their boards. Freestyle was an instant hit! Before long, people from all over the country traveled to Lake Tahoe to witness this new boarding style in action.

RACE IT!

Snowboarding competitions were attracting riders from around the world by the early 1980s. The best riders soon became pros, appearing in magazines and on TV. Many ski resorts, which had previously refused to allow snowboarders on their ski slopes, decided to open their hills to snowboarders. The sport's popularity exploded in the late 1990s with the creation of the **X Games**. In 1998, snowboarding attracted huge crowds during its first appearance at the Olympic Winter Games in Nagano, Japan. Today, snowboarding is a favorite winter sport with athletes of all ages.

TIME LINE

1965: Sherman Poppen invents the Snurfer

1970s: Snurfer competitions are held regularly in Michigan

1975: Dimitrije Milovich begins to manufacture another style of board called the Winterstick

1980: a plastic coating called **P-tex**, used in ski manufacturing, is added to snowboards, making them faster and more challenging to ride

1983: two major snowboarding competitions—the **National Snowboarding Championships** in Vermont and the **World Snowboarding Championships** in California—are organized for the first time

1985: the first snowboarding magazine, Absolutely Radical, is published

1988: the **United States Amateur Snowboarding Association** (USASA) is formed to host safe, fair, and fun amateur competitions

1998: Canadian rider Ross Rebagliati makes history when he wins the very first Olympic gold medal for snowboarding

2002: the USASA hosts the largest snowboarding event in history—the National Championships in Mammoth, California

the Snurfer

7

BOARD NEWS

The first wooden snowboards were very heavy—most weighed over 10 pounds (4.5 kg)! Today's boards are made of more durable materials that can withstand rough rides. Each style of snowboarding requires a different board. The different styles help protect riders from injuries.

BOARD BASICS

The body of a snowboard is made up of different layers. All boards have an inner **core**, or center, made either of foam or of thin planks of wood that have been glued together. The core is covered with **fiberglass**, which makes the board lightweight but strong. The bottom of the board is then coated with P-tex so it will slide over the snow. Sharp strips of metal are **embedded** along the outside edges of the board. They cause the board to cut into the snow, allowing riders to **carve**, or perform smooth, wide turns.

ALPINE BOARDS

The alpine board is designed to give a rider the ultimate carving experience as he or she races downhill. The board has to be very stiff to handle the high speeds reached during a race. Its long, narrow outline provides a racer with the speed and tight turns needed to win. An alpine racer has the board's edges sharpened often to make them cut into the snow during turns. The board's **tail** is flat and is often **tapered**, which means it is not as wide as the **nose**. A tapered board turns more easily. Unfortunately, only a few companies manufacture alpine boards.

*The top of the board is called the **deck**.*

*The bottom of the board is called the **base**. A rider regularly applies **snowboard wax** to the base of his or her board to make it more slippery. Waxing increases a board's speed as it slides over the snow.*

FREESTYLE BOARDS

A freestyle board is tough but flexible, so it won't break when a rider performs tricks. Both the nose and tail of a freestyle board curve upward. The board's **outline**, or shape, is called a **twin-tip** because it has the same rounded shape at both ends. The twin-tip design and curved tail allows a rider to turn and ride the board **fakie**, or with the back foot pointing forward.

FREERIDE BOARDS

A freeride board can take a rider anywhere. Although it is not as wide as a freestyle board, a freeride board is still flexible enough for tricks. A rider can also take to the mountain on this board. Its long outline and wide, upturned nose help a rider make great turns. Many **boardercross** athletes compete on freeride boards because they are so **versatile**.

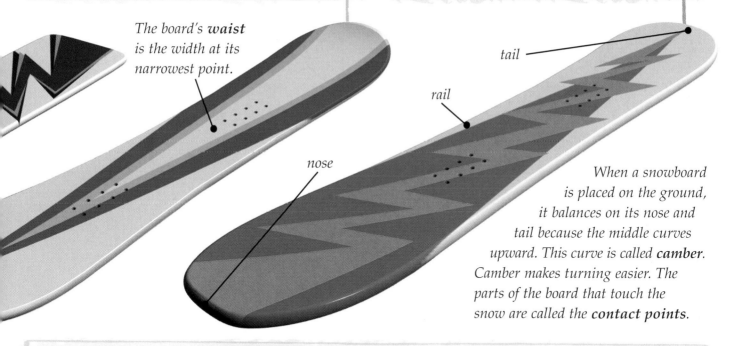

*The board's **waist** is the width at its narrowest point.*

tail

rail

nose

*When a snowboard is placed on the ground, it balances on its nose and tail because the middle curves upward. This curve is called **camber**. Camber makes turning easier. The parts of the board that touch the snow are called the **contact points**.*

CUT IT OUT

The sides of a board are called **rails**. Most rails are not straight. Instead, they curve inward. This curve is known as the board's **sidecut**. Deep sidecuts allow a rider to make sharp turns at slow speeds. A freestyle board often has a deep sidecut. If a board has a shallow sidecut, it can turn sharply at very high speeds. An alpine board has a shallow sidecut.

GEAR UP

Every style of snowboarding presents riders with risky challenges. Snowboarders have to put on a lot of gear and accessories before hitting the slopes. Protective gear helps ensure that every ride is safe and fun.

Every snowboarder falls down sometimes. A thick pair of waterproof gloves keeps a rider's hands warm and protects his or her hands during a fall.

IT'S COLD OUT THERE!

Snowboarders have to wear several layers of clothing to keep warm in the winter weather. If the day warms up, a layer of clothing can simply be removed! Layered clothing also adds padding to help make falls easier on the body. **Thermal** underwear, socks, and a fleece sweater trap body heat and keep a rider dry. This clothing layer should be covered by a waterproof jacket and snow pants.

Most body heat is lost through the head, so many riders wear winter hats.

helmet   goggles

HELMET HEADS

A snowboarder travels at very high speeds, so a helmet is the most important piece of equipment he or she wears. A snowboarding helmet is made to be strong but lightweight. The outer shell is usually hard plastic. The inside is made of foam. A rider has to wear **goggles** to protect his or her eyes from shards of ice and snow. Goggles can prevent **snow blindness** and block dangerous **ultraviolet rays** as well. Riders have to make sure that they purchase goggles that fit over their helmets.

Snowboarders wear plastic wrist, elbow, and knee pads to reduce the risk of fractures and sprains.

highback binding

soft boot

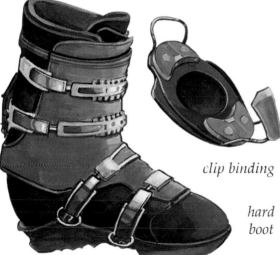

clip binding

hard boot

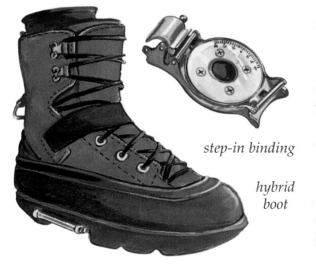

step-in binding

hybrid boot

BOOT IT, BIND IT

Snowboarding boots are among the most important pieces of equipment a snowboarder uses. The boots must fit properly to protect a rider's feet and ankles as he or she performs daring turns and tricks. A good pair of boots will also keep a rider's feet warm and dry.

SOFT BOOTS

Freestyle and some freeride boarders wear soft flexible boots. They are made of leather and **synthetic**, or artificial, materials. Soft boots usually attach to the snowboard with **highback bindings**, which have straps that wrap around the boots.

HARD BOOTS

Alpine racers need hard boots that support their ankles during high-speed turns. These boots have thick plastic outer shells. Metal **clip bindings** secure the boot at the toe and heel. Unfortunately, it can be difficult to find clip bindings in stores.

HYBRID BOOTS

The newest kind of boot is the **hybrid.** It combines elements of soft and hard boots. Hybrid boots are flexible around the top but are firm at the sole. Many hybrid boots use **step-in bindings**. When a rider presses down on the binding with his or her foot, the boot is locked in place.

ALPINE COMPETITIONS

Alpine snowboarding events are timed competitions. Each race is fast-paced and technically challenging. To take part, riders need to have great endurance, flexibility, and strength. They carve down courses that are marked by **gates**, or pairs of poles that hold triangular panels between them. Athletes are **disqualified** if they fail to carve around a gate during a competition. While racing, riders reach speeds of up to 45 miles (72 km) per hour! Some alpine riders wear skintight suits to reduce **drag**, or the resistance that is created when the wind catches loose clothing.

SAFETY FIRST

Traveling at such high speeds can be risky. Safety gear is a must for all alpine racers. They can be seriously injured if they hit a hard plastic gate pole or crash while turning. Alpine racers often wear helmets with **visors**, or face shields. Tough plastic guards are also worn over the shins, arms, hands, and other body parts that could be injured during a fall.

As alpine riders navigate a race course, the intense speed often forces them to hold their bodies almost parallel to the ground.

TRAINING DAYS

Alpine snowboarding requires a rider to
make precise moves. While training, riders
often practice on many kinds of alpine
courses so they will be prepared to handle
unexpected situations during competitions.
It takes years of training for a snowboarder
to achieve the level of fitness and skill
necessary to perform in an alpine race.

AND THEY'RE OFF!

Nothing tests a racer's skill and dedication like competing against other athletes. Alpine riders look forward to the challenge of trying to beat their competitors' best times. There are two main types of alpine competitions— **slalom** and **giant slalom**.

SLALOM

Slalom races have many gates that are placed close together. The two poles of a slalom gate are different heights—one is short and the other is tall. The short pole allows a speeding racer to pass the gate without making contact. Riders must execute very tight turns in order to make it around every gate. They use their instincts to choose the fastest **line**, or path, around the gates. Each rider races in two runs. The overall winner is the racer with the shortest combined time from both races.

GIANT SLALOM

Giant slalom courses are a little different than those used in regular slalom. They are often much longer and, therefore, more difficult to complete. Riders also travel at higher speeds because the gates are placed farther apart. Each rider races in two runs, and the final winner is the rider with the fastest combined time.

Parallel giant slalom races are also very popular. In these races, two riders compete at the same time. It would be much too dangerous for them to share a course, however. Instead, two similar courses are set up next to each other. Both riders perform a timed run on each of the two courses. The final winner is the rider with the best combined time.

FEELING FREE

Freestyle snowboarders create high-flying moves that thrill spectators and encourage competition. Along with many other extreme athletes, snowboarders were inspired by the fast-paced action of freestyle skateboarding. Freestyle snowboarding continues to evolve as today's pros develop new tricks and improve old favorites. Much of freestyle riding is about **getting air**, or being airborne, but many complex tricks are built from a few basic moves.

THE OLLIE

The **ollie** (shown below) is an important freestyle move. To begin, the rider gains some speed while moving in a straight line. He or she then crouches down and pops up from the tail, pulling the board off the ground. If the rider pops up from the nose instead of the tail, this trick is called a **nollie**.

THE BONK

Once riders can perform ollies, they can **bonk**! To bonk, a rider pulls his or her board off the ground and hits it against an object such as a tree or railing.

FAKIE RIDING

Fakie riding is an essential move in freestyle. Riding backward can be hard to get used to, but boarders must master fakie riding before they can hit the halfpipe. Also, tricks performed fakie are more impressive!

THE LOWDOWN ON LINGO

Snowboarders use some creative terms to describe their sport. Here are a few terms that all riders should know:

stance: a rider's body position on the board
regular: a stance that puts the left foot on the nose and the right foot on the tail; most riders are regular
goofy: a stance that puts the right foot on the nose and the left foot on the tail

sick: describes something that is very good
wack: describes something that is very bad
jibbing: riding a snowboard on something other than snow, such as railings or logs
tuck: describes a crouched position used to reduce drag
pipe dragon: a machine used to carve halfpipes out of snow
boned: describes a move that is performed with great emphasis; to bone the leg during a trick means to straighten it as much as possible

Basic tricks help riders improve their technique. Eventually, they can get enough air to perform dazzling tricks.

RIDING THE PIPE

Riders need to get as much air as they can to perform difficult freestyle moves. The halfpipe opens a whole world of tricks to advanced snowboarders. Halfpipes are designed to launch riders straight up into the air. They have two steep sloping sides called **transitions**. Halfpipe transitions face each other, forming a U-shaped ditch. A **quarter-pipe** is a ramp with only one transition. The top edge of a transition is called the **lip** or **coping**. When a rider uses the lip to perform a trick, the move is called a **lip trick**. Halfpipes can be up to 15 feet (5 m) high. The newest halfpipe used in competitions is the **superpipe**. The walls of the superpipe can be up to 18 feet (6 m) high!

AERIAL ACROBATICS

The halfpipe tests a rider's creativity— and guts! Some of the most exciting tricks performed in the halfpipe are **aerials** such as **grabs**, **spins**, and **inverts**. Riders must have great balance and coordination to perform these daring moves.

GRABS

Riders can add grab tricks to make their aerials more difficult and impressive. To perform a grab, the rider takes hold of part of his or her board while in midair. Two common grabs are the **mute** and the **method**. To do a mute, the rider grabs the **toe-edge** of the board in front of the front foot. To do a method, shown above, the rider bends backward and grabs the **heel-edge** of the board with the front hand, pulling it level with his or her head.

SPINS

To spin, a rider turns around in the air before landing. A spin is named for the number of times a rider rotates in the air. A half turn is called a **180** because the rider turns 180°. A full turn is called a **360** because the rider turns 360°. Some pros can even complete a **1080** spin, which is three full rotations!

INVERTS

Invert tricks are challenging. To perform an invert, riders launch themselves into the air and turn their bodies upside down before quickly righting themselves. Riders have to make sure they regain their landing positions before reaching the lip of the pipe! One kind of invert trick is called a **handplant**. To perform a handplant, the rider places one hand on the lip of the pipe and then balances his or her weight on it upside down!

A handplant tests a rider's strength and balance. This snowboarder is combining her handplant with a grab trick.

PARK PLACE

In the early days of snowboarding, riders gained a bad reputation at resorts. They had nowhere to practice freestyle tricks except on public property, which soon became damaged. Many resorts now have **snowparks.** Snowparks are areas filled with **obstacles**, or objects. Here, riders can let their imaginations run wild. By experimenting, they develop their instincts and their individual riding styles. Most parks offer ramps, jumps, and railings in many sizes. A large variety of obstacles gives freestyle riders endless opportunities to improve their skills and to pull off new tricks.

MAKE SOME NOISE

Snowparks are great places for riders to practice **grind** tricks. To perform a grind, the rider slides the board down the length of an obstacle such as a railing. Initially, grinds were skateboarding tricks. Skateboarders named the trick after the noise a board makes as it scrapes along an obstacle's surface. A common grind is the **50-50**. To perform this grind, the rider slides along a railing with only half the board on the obstacle.

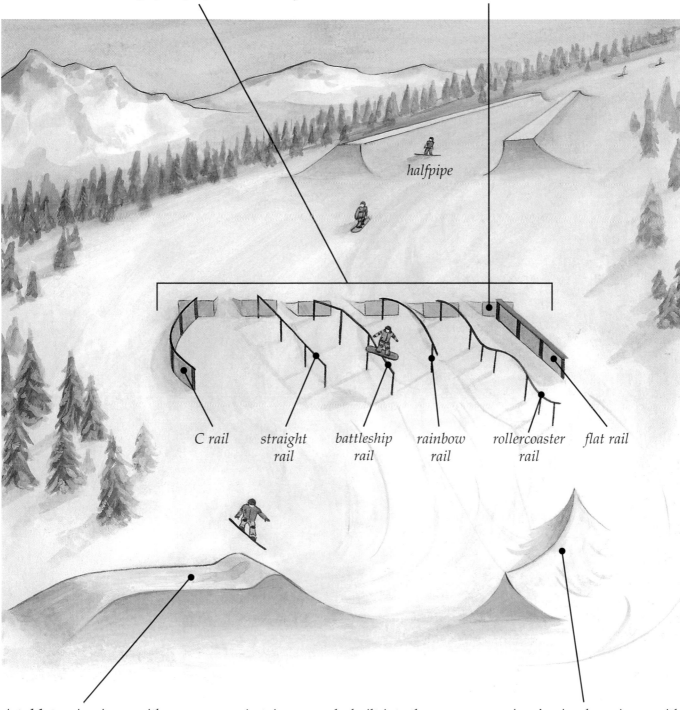

Snowparks often have railings in a variety of shapes for riders to try.

A **kicker** is a smaller jump that leads to another obstacle.

halfpipe

C rail straight rail battleship rail rainbow rail rollercoaster rail flat rail

A **tabletop** is a jump with a flat top. Riders can land on the top or jump over it.

A staircase can be built into the snow to allow boarders to ride a railing or a slippery set of steps.

A **spine** is a large jump with a narrow ridge at the top. Spines are great for tricks.

COMPETING FREESTYLE

Freestyle competitions are awesome displays of creativity and determination. Each year, the best pros and up-and-comers gather for pro and amateur competitions that draw huge crowds of spectators. A panel of judges scores each athlete's **run**, or routine. To get a good score, the riders have to perfect many challenging tricks. The rider with the highest score wins the competition. There are three main styles of freestyle competitions—**slopestyle**, halfpipe, and **big-air**.

SLOPESTYLE

Slopestyle competitions are showcases for the latest freestyle tricks. A competition is performed on a course filled with obstacles usually found in a snowpark. The land between each obstacle is flat, which allows riders to gain speed between tricks. Riders attempt the course one at a time. They are judged on their creativity, style, and how well they use the course.

RULE THE PIPE

Halfpipe competitions are the most popular snowboarding events. The pros perform in the pipe individually. Each run is scored by a panel of five judges. Competitors attempt very difficult spins and inverts (shown below) to impress the judges. Each run lasts only a few minutes, so riders have to make every trick count. They often use **combinations**, or tricks that are executed one right after the other.

BIGGER IS BETTER

Big-air competitors have a lot of nerve! These high-flying athletes thrill spectators as they tear down a steep hill one at a time and finally launch themselves from a giant ramp. The riders then perform tricks while in midair. When scoring a competition, the judges consider which jumper had the best height, distance, and landing, as well as the most difficult tricks.

23

FREERIDING FUN

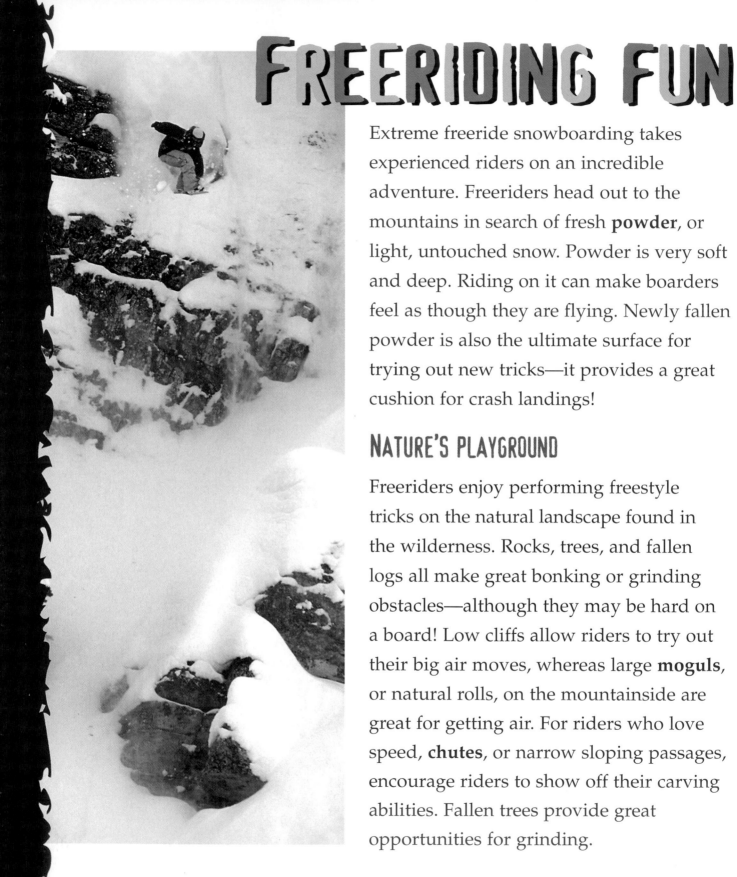

Extreme freeride snowboarding takes experienced riders on an incredible adventure. Freeriders head out to the mountains in search of fresh **powder**, or light, untouched snow. Powder is very soft and deep. Riding on it can make boarders feel as though they are flying. Newly fallen powder is also the ultimate surface for trying out new tricks—it provides a great cushion for crash landings!

NATURE'S PLAYGROUND

Freeriders enjoy performing freestyle tricks on the natural landscape found in the wilderness. Rocks, trees, and fallen logs all make great bonking or grinding obstacles—although they may be hard on a board! Low cliffs allow riders to try out their big air moves, whereas large **moguls**, or natural rolls, on the mountainside are great for getting air. For riders who love speed, **chutes**, or narrow sloping passages, encourage riders to show off their carving abilities. Fallen trees provide great opportunities for grinding.

SAFETY FIRST

Freeriding isn't all fun, however. Riders should never travel alone into the backcountry. They need to bring a lot of equipment for their trips up the mountain. A compass, watch, shovel, and **avalanche bleeper** are all necessary. Deep snow can hide rocks, **tree wells**, and other unseen obstacles that can cause injuries. A rider may also need help if he or she is caught in an **avalanche**, or a wall of snow and ice that falls suddenly down a mountain. Listening to the weather report before heading out for a freeride experience is always a must!

Riders have to hike up steep mountainsides before they can enjoy the ride down.

BOARDER X

Boardercross or "snowboard cross" is a new snowboarding competition that is popular in North America, Europe, Australia, and New Zealand. The name boardercross is a combination of the words snowboarding and **motocross**, a motorcycle sport in which a group of riders races on an outdoor course. Boardercross combines the breathtaking tricks of freestyle with the extreme speed of an alpine race. During a competition, up to six competitors battle **simultaneously**, or at the same time, for the lead position. The first

three riders to cross the finish line from each group advance to the next round. The course is loaded with obstacles that test each rider's coordination, balance, and ability to strategize his or her next move quickly. A rider's performance at the start of a race is key to winning. Boardercross courses are narrow, so crashes often involve many riders. The racer who bursts out in front from the starting gate usually avoids crashes and wins the race.

Boardercross will be an official event in the 2006 Olympic Winter Games.

A RACE TO THE FINISH

Boardercross courses are challenging for riders because they have so many obstacles—and so much competition! **Whoop-de-doos** or "whoops" are a series of jumps placed one after the other. Riders can jump the whoops or attempt to slide right over them.

Berms are other common obstacles on a boardercross course. A berm is a **banked**, or angled, corner. Berms can reduce a rider's speed if they are not handled correctly. Most courses also include a variety of tabletops and **double-jumps**, or two large jumps placed one after the other.

Boardercross riders try to avoid getting too much air off the jumps because they lose speed while they're in the air. They stay as close to the ground as they can.

FAMOUS SNOWBOARDERS

Many dedicated athletes have worked very hard to make extreme snowboarding as thrilling as it is today. Every year, the pros bring snowboarding to a new level through their dedication and tireless practice. These pages include just a few of the riders who have had a major impact on their sport.

TERJE HAAKENSON

Norwegian boarder Terje Haakenson is the king of this sport. Considered by most people to be the best rider in the world, Haakenson has won the European halfpipe championship a remarkable five times, the U.S. Open three times, and the Mt. Baker Banked Slalom competition four times! Already a legend at the age of 26, Haakenson will certainly continue to amaze crowds for years to come with his unbelievable skill.

SHANNON DUNN

American Shannon Dunn (shown above) started snowboarding in 1998 and turned pro just two years later. Dunn has been dominating halfpipe competitions for years, and she's also an accomplished slopestyle competitor. She has many first-place titles and has even won a bronze medal at the 1998 Olympic Games.

CRAIG KELLY

Snowboarding lost a legend in 2003, when American rider Craig Kelly died. He was a founder of the sport and went on to be crowned world champion four times and U.S. Open champion three times, while also winning dozens of other competitions. An inspiration to every pro, Kelly is considered one of the best snowboarders of all time.

LESLEY MCKENNA

British rider Lesley McKenna raced to star status, becoming one of the top five boarders in the world just six years after first strapping on a snowboard. Although she was a skier in her youth, McKenna turned to snowboarding at age 20 and was soon winning halfpipe and boardercross competitions. A founder of the British Women's Snowboarding Team, she strives to give British riders a chance to shine.

ROSS POWERS

American rider Ross Powers has few equals. He was a sponsored rider by the age of nine! Powers is almost unbeatable in halfpipe competitions—he's won every championship at least once! After appearing in several snowboarding films and documentaries, Powers' popularity can only grow.

American rider Craig Kelly was a pioneer of snowboarding.

JUMP ON BOARD

Feel like joining the fun? Snowboarding is a great activity for people of all ages. Riders can stay in shape while enjoying the inspiring sights of the great outdoors. It is important to remember, however, that snowboarding is a challenging sport. You can be injured if you try difficult moves before you've mastered the basics. Also, you should never snowboard without wearing the proper safety equipment. A helmet and pads must be worn at all times. Beginners will want to use a **leash**, which attaches the snowboard to the ankle. A leash is helpful if you wipe out—your board won't fly up and hit another rider, and it will be easy for you to find.

THE WAY TO BEHAVE

Snowboarders must remember that they share the slopes with other athletes. Riders travel at high speeds, and they can put others and themselves in danger if they do not ride responsibly. Never cut off another rider or a skier. Stopping suddenly on a slope is also very dangerous!

Never snowboard alone! If you find yourself lost, injured, or simply worn out, you'll want a friend around to help you get home.

FINDING HELP

Snowboarding is a lot more fun when you feel confident on your board. Learning from a trained instructor or coach is the best way to ensure that you'll handle a board with skill. An instructor can teach you valuable safety tips, such as how to **bail**, or fall, properly without getting hurt. Snowboarding magazines, such as *TransWorld Snowboarding*, will keep you up-to-date on equipment and all the competitions. It might also be helpful to visit a local snowboard shop to chat with the dealers and perhaps meet some experienced riders. The Internet is always a useful tool for those who want to learn. Here are a few sites to get you started:

www.usasa.org—the official site of the United States of America Snowboarding Association
www.transworldsnowboarding.com/snow—detailed articles and the latest news about everything to do with snowboarding
www.snowboarding.com—product reviews, photos, news, and a lot more

GLOSSARY

Note: Boldfaced words that are defined in the text may not appear in the glossary.

aerials Tricks performed in midair

avalanche bleeper Equpiment that creates a loud noise to help people locate a rider who has been buried in an avalanche

backcountry An area with few inhabitants

binding Equipment that attaches a rider's boots to a snowboard

boardercross A snowboarding competition in which six riders compete at the same time

disqualify To force a rider who has broken the rules to leave a competition

embed To fix firmly around a solid mass

fiberglass A material made from glass fibers

heel-edge The side of a snowboard that a rider's heels face

ski technology Scientific methods used in ski manufacturing

snow blindness A temporary loss of vision caused by exposure to very bright sunlight reflected from snow or ice

snowboard wax A thick substance that is melted onto the base of a snowboard

sponsor To pay an athlete money to use a company's equipment or to wear its clothing

thermal Describes clothing that is designed to keep in body heat

toe-edge The side of the snowboard that a rider's toes face

tree wells Pockets of air that form beneath the snow between trees and can trap fallen riders

X Games An annual series of extreme sports competitions

ultraviolet rays Invisible waves of light that can cause cancer

versatile Capable of being used in many ways

INDEX

1 2 3 4 5 6 7 8 9 0   Printed in the U.S.A.   3 2 1 0 9 8 7 6 5 4